MW01231005

Los Angeles Quake: 1994

Rich Smith

Published by Abdo & Daughters, 4940 Viking Dr., Suite 622, Edina, MN 55435.

Library bound edition distributed by Rockbottom Books, Pentagon Tower, P.O. Box 36036, Minneapolis, Minnesota 55435.

Cover Photo by: AP/Wide World Photos
Inside Photos by: AP/Wide World Photos: 9, 11, 12, 17, 19
Reuters/Bettman: 3, 5, 10, 13, 18, 20, 23, 24, 26, 28, 29

Edited By John Hamilton

LIBRARY OF CONGRESS CATALOGING-IN-PUBLICATION DATA

Smith, Rich, 1954
    L.A. Quake, 1994 / Rich Smith.
      p.   cm. -- (Day of the Disaster)
    Includes bibliographical references and index.
    ISBN 1-56239-320-0
    1. Earthquakes--California--Los Angeles--Juvenile literature.
2. Los Angeles (Calif.)--Histroy--Juvenile literature.
[1. Earthquakes--California--Los Angeles. 2.Los Angeles (Calif.)--History.] I. Title. II. Title: L.A. Quake. 1994. III. Series.
F869.L857S58 1994   94-9661
979.4'94053--dc20   CIP
                      AC

National Guard troops with M-16 rifles patrol along Hollywood Boulevard in Hollywood, California, after the January 17 Los Angeles earthquake.

3

Los Angeles Quake: 1994

In the dark of night on Jan. 17, 1994, a fierce earthquake rocked the sleeping city of Los Angeles, California.

The terrifying shaker lasted just 30 seconds. But it measured magnitude 6.8 on the Richter Scale. It was the most destructive earthquake yet to strike America's second largest city.

But it was not the dreaded Big One. The Big One will be a quake registering magnitude 8.0 or higher. It still lurks somewhere in the future.

This time, 60 people died. Nearly 8,000 were injured. At least 20,000 fled to emergency shelters.

Hundreds of buildings lay in crumpled heaps, and thousands of others were made unsafe to enter. Underground natural gas pipelines broke and exploded in giant fireballs. Sections of vital highways were destroyed. Electricity was knocked out as far away as Wyoming and Canada.

So serious was the damage that officials called L.A.'s Martin Luther King Day Earthquake the costliest natural disaster ever for the United States.

Half of an expensive home lies in ruin after the earthquake caused a landslide.

(Here is the story of that day—as told by a fictional geology research scientist writing in her diary.)

Friday, Dec. 24, 1993

What a great Christmas present from the National Science Foundation! The organization said it's going to pay for a study of how earthquakes affect different neighborhoods here in Los Angeles. We could learn a lot from such an investigation. The findings might help us save lives and buildings in future earthquakes.

We know that earthquakes have a starting point and then move outward in waves. These shock waves can grow weaker or stronger as they pass through different kinds of soil and rock. That's why a quake can sometimes be worse miles away from where it started. Some neighborhoods are built over ground that absorbs and muffles earthquake waves. Others are built over ground that reflect them, making them stronger.

Thursday, Dec. 30

The National Science Foundation study comes at a good time for another reason. We have lately discovered a web of very dangerous fault lines hidden under the Los Angeles area. Faults are what trigger earthquakes. We think one or more of these faults may be getting ready to produce a real shaker.

But what is disturbing to us about these newly discovered faults is that the ground might not jerk from side to side, which is what happens in most earthquakes. Instead, the ground probably will jolt up and down, which makes the potential for death and destruction so much greater.

The Richter Scale

Some earthquakes are stronger than others. Scientists have a way to measure the strength of each one. They use the Richter Scale.

The Richter Scale was invented by Charles Richter. He spent his entire life trying to understand how earthquakes happen.

The scale begins at zero and stops at 10, although theoretically there is no upper limit to the scale. Destructive earthquakes usually measure 5 or higher. Each number up the scale means the earthquake shook 10 times harder than the number just before it. So, an earthquake measured at 6.0 is 10 times stronger than an earthquake measured at 5.0. And it's 100 times stronger than an earthquake measured at 4.0, and 1,000 times stronger than an earthquake measured at 3.0.

10

9

8 — A "great" earthquake. Tremendous damage.

7 — A major earthquake. Widespread, heavy damage.

6 — Severe damage.

5 — Considerable damage.

4 — Moderate damage.

— A quake of magnitude 3.5 can cause slight damage.

3

2

1933 Japan: **8.9**
1906 San Francisco Earthquake: **8.3**
1985 Mexico City: **8.1**
1989 Loma Prieta (San Francisco): **7.1**
1994 *Los Angeles: 7.0*
1971 Sylmar: **6.4**

1

0

Magnitude

The 1994 Los Angeles Earthquake measured nearly 7.0. The strongest earthquake ever measured was nearly 9.0. It happened in Japan in 1933.

What would it be like in an earthquake that measured 10 on the Richter Scale? Scientists say not a single building would remain standing in the area closest to the center of the earthquake.

7

Sunday, Jan. 9, 1994
3:01 p.m.

A magnitude 3.7 earthquake has occurred in the Pacific Ocean just off-shore from the beach city of Santa Monica to the immediate west of Los Angeles. The quake wasn't strong enough to do more than rattle dishes and set off burglar alarms. But it was the first quake we've felt in the Los Angeles area in 18 months.

The standard procedure after a quake this size or greater is for police, fire and rescue units to take to the streets and look for signs of damage. They did, and found none. Thank goodness.

10:12 p.m.

A second quake has been reported in the same area. This one was some-what milder. It measured 3.1 on the Richter Scale and lasted only about five seconds.Our instruments showed that each quake was an up-and-down jolt, which is exactly what we've feared.

Tuesday, Jan. 11
11:27 p.m.

Yet another minor earthquake struck, again in the same location at sea. This one measured 3.5 on the Richter Scale.

Wednesday, Jan. 12
11:28 a.m.

A fourth earthquake has been recorded. Our seismometers registered it at magnitude 3.2.

It's very rare to have quakes in a swarm like this. But we don't think it's a sign of a much bigger quake heading our way. Minor earthquakes usually act as a safety valve to gradually relieve underground pressure along the fault lines. This lessens the chances of the earth lurching might-ily all at once. So, perhaps this rash of little quakes is a good thing.

Residents climb down a hill under a house damaged in Malibu, California.

Even so, many citizens are becoming quite nervous. A few are worried enough to have purchased earthquake survival kits. Maybe I should play it safe and check to see if my quake kit is properly stocked with food, water, bandages, medicine, sanitation supplies, blankets, leather work gloves, fresh batteries, a portable radio and tools. These items will be crucial in the event of a major earthquake.

Monday, Jan. 17, 1994
4:31 a.m.

I was sound asleep. Without any warning, the house began to shudder violently. It was like the place was being thumped up and down on the knee of an angry giant. This quake was much, much more powerful than any of those in the swarm a few days earlier. I guessed it was at least

Many freeways and overpasses collapsed, blocking traffic and slowing down rescue efforts.

magnitude 6. It would take 2 million NASA space shuttles blasting off all at once to equal the energy of a magnitude 6 earthquake!

Dishes flew out of cabinets and crashed to the floor. Heavy wood dinner tables, sofas, beds and everything in the house was thrown through the air. Windows shattered with explosive force. Broken glass was everywhere. The doors snapped off of their hinges. The house bucked and twisted. It was impossible to stand up without being knocked to the floor. Huge cracks formed on the walls. Vast chunks of plaster fell from the ceilings and thick blankets of dust filled the air.

A man watches as his friend's home goes up in flames at the Oak Ridge Trailer Park in Sylmar, California.

At that point I could no longer see what was happening—the lights flick-ered and went black. There was only deafening noise. Then I felt a blast of wind—it was part of the house collapsing! I thought to myself I've got to get out before the rest of it falls on top of me! But suddenly the shak-ing stopped and all was calm again.

The first thing I checked for was the odor of natural gas. Earthquakes often cause gas pipes to snap open. That creates a danger of fire from an accidental spark. Sure enough, the odor of natural gas was thick in the air. I reached the main shut-off valve leading into the house in time to prevent a blaze.

Down the street, a neighbor was not so fortunate. What remained of his house after the quake was finished off by a massive mushroom of flame. And in the distance, the night sky took on an orange glow. I couldn't begin to guess how many other homes across the city were burning.

A fireman looks desperately for water as the Oak Ridge Trailer Park in the Sylmar section of the San Fernando Valley burns.

A police officer stands on top of a car alongside a section of freeway that collapsed during the earthquake.

(The story is picked up from here with this account by a fictional rescue worker. He recorded the following observations on tape.)

5 a.m.

The Los Angeles Emergency Response system has been activated. Thousands of off-duty police, fire fighters, paramedics and rescue workers are mobilizing. As soon as we receive our orders, we will begin fanning out across the region in search of trouble and people in need of help.

But we're off to a bad start. Several police precinct buildings have been evacuated because of damage. And at some fire stations, the hook-and-ladder units can't get out because their garage doors are jammed shut.

The emergency response system is directed from a command post in an earthquake-proof room, four floors beneath City Hall. I'm here with about 30 disaster officials and their aides from city, county and state government. One important person who has not yet arrived is Los Angeles Chief of Police Willie Williams. We have word that his home was badly damaged and that a tall cabinet made of heavy wood toppled onto his bed. It missed him by an inch. He might have been killed had it come any closer and hit him. The chief was very fortunate.

5:50 a.m.

There aren't enough fire fighters and fire engines available in the city to battle all the flames. The fire chief is on the phone calling the chiefs all around the state to request help. The ones who don't have too much earthquake damage of their own are going to send us spare equipment and fire fighters.

6:45 a.m.

We've just learned that 350 search-and-rescue workers from outside the area have begun pouring into the city. The official who is coordinating their activities says the people affected by the quake shout cheers to the rescuers as they arrive.

14

7 a.m.

It has taken a long time for the damage reports to flow in. It seems the quake wiped out a large part of our emergency communications network. But we're now getting through to enough of our people on the outside to sketch a rough picture of the situation.

"It looks like we have damage everywhere," Police Commission President Gary Greenebaum has declared. The worst of it appears to be in the San Fernando Valley on the city's north side and in Santa Monica to the west.

More than a dozen major highways are buckled. Out on Interstate 10—the Santa Monica Freeway—seven concrete support columns gave way and allowed an overpass to collapse onto Fairfax Avenue below. This is very, very bad because the Santa Monica Freeway is the nation's busiest highway. Some 300,000 commuters and truckers use it every day to drive in and out of downtown Los Angeles. Without this main artery, traffic in the city could become a nightmare. A 30-minute drive to work might now take several hours. The engineers already on the scene say the freeway could be out of service a year or longer. Not good news at all.

The police set up barricades to stop cars from getting on the freeway. While they were in the process of doing that, one motorist drove right on past. He didn't get far, though. There was a huge slab of concrete jutting up like a wall from the broken roadbed. He didn't see it so he smashed right into it. The police had to call for an ambulance to take him to the hospital. Meanwhile, a bridge on Interstate 5 near Sylmar collapsed. And so did one on the Antelope Valley Freeway—Highway 14. These are the two main roads used by most of the 130,000 people of the suburban Santa Clarita Valley to travel to jobs in Los Angeles.

There was tragedy on the Antelope Valley Freeway. A Los Angeles Police officer on a motorcycle couldn't tell that the overpass ahead was gone. Clarence Wayne Dean sailed over the road's sudden end and dropped 30 feet to his death.

Three travelers on Interstate 5 were far more fortunate. The quake completely ripped through the beginning and end portions of the bridge that crosses Old Road. The middle section of the bridge stayed up. This caused the drivers of a big-rig truck, a motorhome and a pick-up to become stranded 60 feet in the air. They was no way to climb down from that perch. So the three people had to be airlifted off.

7:30 a.m.

We hear that many hospitals are evacuating their sick. So far about 1,000 patients have been taken out of at least three hospitals in the area where the quake seems to have hit hardest. The worst damage is at Olive View Medical Center. Water pipes have ruptured all through the building, and gas fumes are everywhere. Olive View was supposed to be able to withstand an earthquake. It was destroyed once before by a temblor and rebuilt in 1971 using advanced "quake-safe" construction techniques.

Meanwhile, hospitals that survived are being swamped by injured people. At Cedars-Sinai Hospital near West Hollywood, the doctors are reporting a "tidal wave of walking wounded" in need of treatment. The most common injury is for cuts. Many people were cut by flying glass from windows. Others were cut when they got out of bed and walked barefoot in the dark over floors covered with bits of broken dishes, glass and splintered wood.

7:44 a.m.

Natural gas pipelines ruptured beneath streets in some parts of the city as soon as the quake struck. In the Sylmar district of the San Fernando Valley, 64 homes exploded in flames fed from a buried pipeline. One of the homes held a stockpile of ammunition: the fire sent bullets whizzing every which way. Fire fighters said it was like being in a war zone. They also discovered there wasn't enough water pressure in the hydrants for them to easily hose down the flames. That's a sign that underground water mains were broken, too.

On Balboa Boulevard in Granada Hills, an entire neighborhood burned after a frantic driver started the engine of his automobile. It seems his car was sitting atop a broken underground gas pipeline. Escaping gas seeped up through cracks in the pavement and was detonated by a spark from the car's ignition system. The car was destroyed and the driver was very seriously burned. He was on his way to check on his mother. She lived several miles away. But he was so worried about her safety that he ignored his injuries and continued making his way to her home on foot.

7:59 a.m.

Many buildings have collapsed. Much of Cal State University in Northridge was destroyed. The Bullocks department store at the Northridge Fashion Center is now just a pile of twisted steel and rubble.

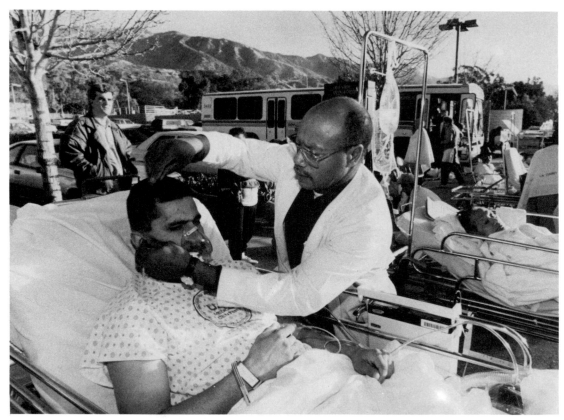

A man is treated for injuries at an emergency unit setup outside Olive View Medical Center in Sylmar, California.

Miles of storefronts and offices along Ventura Boulevard are in shambles. The stadium where the Raiders and USC football teams play their home games is cracked all the way around.

Freight trains hauling poisonous chemicals flipped off their tracks. Los Angeles International Airport has no electricity and is closed to all flights. And telephone circuits are jammed beyond capacity with callers trying to make sure the quake hasn't harmed people elsewhere in the region.

The city is virtually cut off from the rest of the world. Right now, it looks like we're on our own. We as citizens will have to depend on each other for our immediate survival.

A family made homeless by the earthquake sleeps in Reseda Park as evening sets in. Thousands of people were made homeless by the quake.

Rescue workers looking for a missing elderly woman go through the rubble of a home in the Studio City section of Los Angeles.

8:15 a.m.

I've been ordered to assist in the rescue of a man trapped beneath the ruins of a parking structure at Northridge Fashion Center. The victim is Salvador Pena. He is the man who operates the street sweeper that cleans the parking spaces every morning. Pena was just getting started on the lowest level of the parking structure at the time of the quake.

9:30 a.m.

I'm at the scene now. I've been told Pena is in terrible condition. His legs are smashed and they think he has lost a lot of blood. Amazingly, Pena seems in good spirits. We can hear him yelling out to us that he wants us to reach him so we can join him in prayer.

A rescue worker uses an air-bag wedge to lift concrete at the collapsed Northridge Mall parking structure. Each bag can support 72 tons.

The rescue leader has decided to use air-bag wedges to help free Pena. These flattened bags are shoved into crevices under the wall and ceiling slabs that have fallen. Then we pump air into each bag to expand it. This raises the fallen slabs high enough to form a tunnel. Each bag can support 72 tons of weight. We can reach Pena this way. But there is so much concrete on top of him that it will take several hours before he is rescued.

Noon

We're inching closer to Pena. It won't be long for him now. Meanwhile, I just heard on the radio that Governor Pete Wilson has ordered 1,800 National Guard troops to take up positions around the city. Their job will be to help the police stop criminals from breaking in and stealing things from damaged stores.

1 p.m.

Pena has been freed! Everyone is congratulating one another. The cheeks of Fire Captain Jim Vandell are streaked with tears of joy. It's a highly emotional moment.

A helicopter just landed nearby and will fly Pena to UCLA Medical Center for emergency surgery. The doctors can't tell at this point whether or not he'll live.

My orders now are to hurry to the Northridge Meadows apartment building some blocks away at 9565 Reseda Blvd. Crews have been working there all day to rescue a dozen people trapped after the second and third floors crashed down onto the first floor. At least 15 residents so far are known to have been crushed to death. That makes Northridge Meadows the single most tragic location in the city.

1:30 p.m.

I remember passing by the Northridge Meadows building many times in the past. I can hardly believe my eyes. It used to be a beautiful complex of about 160 apartments. Now, parts of the structure have been reduced to an ugly pile of debris.

As I arrive I see that some of the rescuers are trying to comfort a weeping woman. She was in one of the apartments on the first floor. She and her 14-year-old son managed to escape. But her husband and other son remained trapped inside. Their limp bodies were found a short while ago.

1:40 p.m.

Two tenants who also escaped told me how scary it was. One said he thought Godzilla had picked up the building and then hurled it to the ground like a toy. The quake started and then a second or two later everything caved in, said the other. So fast was it that the dead probably never had time to react before they were killed.

2 p.m.

Air-bag wedges again get the credit for helping unearth people pinned within the building. A man who is still trapped has let us know we're getting closer to where he is. "I can see blue sky! I can see blue sky! It's beautiful!" he hollered up to us.

4 p.m.

The chances of finding more survivors beneath the rubble grow smaller with each passing hour. We have been using specially trained dogs to sniff for signs of life. We also have been listening for sounds of movement or cries for help coming from below by aiming super-sensitive microphones at the ruins.

Right now we're getting near the innermost part of the collapse. The debris is so thick and heavy that we're forced to use diamond-bladed saws to chew our way through. It looks like the search-and-rescue efforts here at Northridge Meadows will continue throughout the night and probably into the next day.

4:30 p.m.

The word from command headquarters is that fire fighters have brought many of the city's blazes under control. But Battalion Chief Claude

Creasy tells us he is worried about the danger from earthquake after-shocks. He says many buildings left standing are weakened enough that a good-sized aftershock could make them fall.

Indeed, there have been numerous aftershocks throughout the day. The strongest ones have been much less powerful than the earthquake itself. But they still pack plenty of punch. The children and many grown-ups cry each time the ground trembles.

Firemen stand next to the three-story Northridge Meadows apartment building that collapsed during the earthquake.

Evening

The people who live next door to Northridge Meadows and all along the block as far down as I can see have been camped on the sidewalks. A lot of them look dazed. With the arrival of nightfall, many of the newly homeless have headed for the emergency shelters run by the Red Cross and other disaster agencies. However, some residents have chosen to pitch makeshift tents in the public park. The open spaces somehow feel safer to them than do the walls of the school gymnasium where the shelter is located.

Water is in very short supply. The quake obliterated mains that carry water to many neighborhoods. Some people are able to take water they

A woman fills up a water bottle from a military truck at Granada Hill's Kennedy High School. For days after the quake water throughout the San Fernando Valley was undrinkable.

need from swimming pools, water heaters, cans of vegetables, even the tanks of their toilets. Others have been able to purchase water in bottles from the few open stores here and there. The rest will have to wait for fresh water to be trucked in by disaster relief workers.

Elsewhere, water that is still flowing through pipes has turned brown and is unsafe to drink unless boiled first.

9 p.m.

There was a report on the radio a moment ago that doctors have finished operating on Salvador Pena. It took five hours to patch him up. They said it was a miracle he lived. He's going to be alright! I bet his wife and kids are real happy to hear that!

Tuesday, Jan. 18
Morning

The city has only now begun to realize the true extent of the disaster. Cal Tech reported the quake measured at least 6.6 on the Richter Scale. It was felt up and down California from Mexico to Oregon. The Department of Water and Power said the city was blacked out completely for the first time in its history.

The destruction seems to have hop-scotched around the region. One neighborhood has devastation while the next one has little or none. It was very strange. But that's what scientists warned might happen.

There were many, many stories of personal tragedy and loss. The newspapers reported a number of people died from nothing more than sheer fright. A man plummeted to his doom when the quake catapulted him through a window of his sixth-floor apartment. A mother was killed after she slipped on a toy in the dark and hit her head on the crib of her peacefully sleeping baby. A man was electrocuted as he tried to rescue a small child from a car tangled in fallen power lines. A movie-maker perished when his hillside mansion crashed to the bottom of the slope.

Pets became spooked by the shaking. Many of them ran away from home. Fortunately, kind strangers have been herding lost pets into the city's animal shelters where they are being reunited with their owners.

There was plenty of irony, too. The biggest example was the destruction of the home of Charles Richter. Richter was the man who invented the system for measuring the strength of earthquakes. He died several years ago. But a nephew had turned Richter's home into an earthquake museum. Gone were all of Richter's research papers and inventions, including his first earthquake measuring machine.

Oddly enough, it seems the earthquake also did some good. Broken clocks suddenly started keeping time again. Doors that wouldn't close because they were out of alignment mysteriously became aligned once more. And some people with terrible back aches were instantly cured.

There was even the story of a vacationing family from Australia that planned to go on the earthquake simulation ride at Universal Studios Tour. But after experiencing the real thing Monday, the family wondered why bother? Meanwhile, Los Angeles city schools will be closed all this week so classrooms can be inspected for safety.

President Bill Clinton talks with Department of Water and Power workers January 19 as he tours earthquake-damaged areas in Los Angeles.

Wednesday, Jan. 19
Morning

President Bill Clinton toured the disaster area. The people were really glad to see him. President Clinton, Governor Wilson and Los Angeles Mayor Richard Riordan talked about what needs to be done next to get the city back on its feet. President Clinton promised at least $6 billion in federal aid, and maybe more. Good. We'll need every penny. The damage estimate right now stands between $15 billion and $30 billion, according to the governor.

Afternoon

Relief is arriving from all over the world. Federal officials have been distributing food, water and emergency funds to help people move into undamaged homes and apartments.

The bad news is we're expecting heavy rain in a few days. That's all the newly homeless need now—a drenching. The rain will also make clean-up and repair work more difficult. And there is the danger of flash floods and mudslides because many of the hills surrounding Los Angeles have no trees or plants to catch the rainfall. Those were burned up in last autumn's firestorms.

(The earthquake scientist from Cal Tech concludes the story with these thoughts from her diary)

Thursday, Jan. 20

We've been able to trace the source of the quake by studying data from 270 seismometers scattered across Southern California. The evidence shows it began at a point 10 miles below the Granada Hills district. Then it shot upward at an angle. The full force of the quake reached the surface two miles away on Balboa Boulevard in Granada Hills. It then zig-zagged along the ground for two blocks and created a tear in the earth that ended at Amestoy Avenue and Flanders Street. This was ground-zero. The epicenter.

People had to wait for hours to get paperwork to apply for federal disaster assistance.

The quake raised up parts of Northridge, the Northridge Hills and the Santa Susana Mountains a good foot or two. Meanwhile, the northeast portion of the San Fernando Valley slumped an equal distance.

Tuesday, Feb. 1

My colleagues and I have been giving a lot of thought to something these last few days. The King Day Earthquake occurred along just one branch of a gigantic thrust-fault system. We know it is possible for a single quake to touch off other quakes all at once across an entire thrust-fault system. This hasn't happened yet in Los Angeles. But, if it ever does, it will produce destruction countless times worse than what we've already seen.

The King Day Earthquake was the eighth major temblor to strike Southern California since 1971. There almost certainly will be a ninth at some point in the not-too-distant future. The question is will the next one be like the King Day Earthquake or will it be *the* Big One we've all been fearing? Only time will tell.

Shocked residents watch a building burn in Sherman Oaks, California, following the earthquake.

Glossary

Aftershock

Any shaking of the ground in the minutes, hours, days or weeks following a major earthquake. Most aftershocks are mild, but some can be nearly as strong as the earthquake itself. Aftershocks become fewer and farther apart as time passes. They continue until the pressures on the rocks beneath the earth are relieved.

Epicenter

The location where an earthquake begins. The trembling is at its very strongest there. The shaking moves outward in all directions from that point, just like the ripple when a pebble is dropped into the water of a quiet pond.

Evacuate

To leave someplace quickly because of emergency or danger. Rescuers often have to help people evacuate buildings that become unsafe in an earthquake.

Fault

A miles-long line in the ground where huge sections of the earth's crust join. The sections are constantly pushing against one another. This causes underground pressures to build and build until finally one of the sections suddenly moves several feet. This sudden sideways movement is felt on the ground's surface in the form of an earthquake.

Geologist

A person who studies the earth and its layers of rock and soil.

Magnitude

Greatness of size, power or extent. Earthquakes are measured by their magnitude. Scientists speak of an earthquake's magnitude to describe the force of the shaking.

Seismometer

A special instrument that measures earthquakes. It tells scientists the strength of the earthquake and how long it lasted. Scientists can identify an earthquake's epicenter by comparing measurements from seismometers at locations scattered many miles apart.

Temblor

Spanish word meaning earthquake. People in Los Angeles often use *temblor* in place of *earthquake* because the Spanish language is such an important part of the city's heritage and culture.

Thrust-fault

A special kind of fault in which the underground pressures cause the earth to push up or down instead of sideways. Thrust-faults produce the most dangerous earthquakes in Southern California because most buildings are designed more to survive sideways shaking than up-and-down bumping.

Index